MW01251640

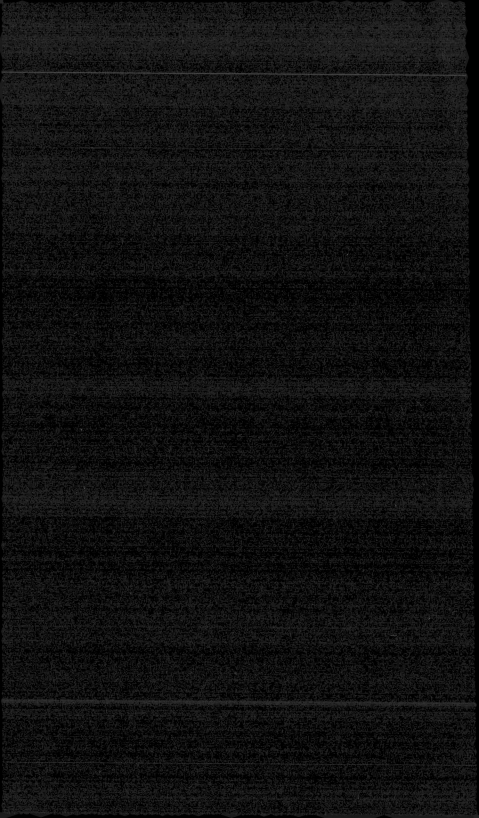

Lady Crawford

Lady Crawford

JULIE CAMERON GRAY

Copyright © 2016 Julie Cameron Gray
All rights reserved

Palimpsest Press
1171 Eastlawn Ave.
Windsor, Ontario. N8S 3J1
www.palimpsestpress.ca

Book and cover design by Dawn Kresan. Typeset in Adobe Garamond
Pro, and printed offset on Rolland Zephyr Laid at Coach House
Printing in Ontario, Canada. Edited by Jim Johnstone.

Palimpsest Press would like to thank the Canada Council for the Arts,
and the Ontario Arts Council for their support of our publishing
program. We also acknowledge the assistance of the Government of
Ontario through the Ontario Book Publishing Tax Credit.

Library and Archives Canada Cataloguing in Publication

Cameron Gray, Julie, author
        Lady Crawford / Julie Cameron Gray.

Poems.
ISBN 978-1-926794-35-8 (paperback)

        I. TITLE.

PS8613.R3877L33 2016   C811'.6   C2016-903806-8

for Guy

Luxury is the wolf at the door and its fangs are the vanities and conceits germinated by success. When an artist learns this, he knows where the dangers lie. Without deprivation and struggle, there is no salvation and I am just a sword cutting daisies.

—TENNESSEE WILLIAMS

Contents

I. LAST TO LEAVE THE PARTY

Last to Leave the Party

where they parse out mountains
as swag, forests
        bundled with deer, cool dark ponds—

            wilderness begging to be owned
            and handled with remote disinterest

as though we were discussing the discovery
            of a new world, vistas of silks and spices
            wrapped in selves that escaped out
            the side door at some soiree years ago.

        Here, the eye's charisma scrapes
        smiles into the potted plants, spires
        of green succulents. So if we must

be our authentic selves, no matter how grim,
let's say the things we came here to say while drunk:

When the layer cake's sediment
        yields up every last fossil of our youth,
            we will have run out of good looks and be left

with a harsh triad, stripped
of all veils:

        regret, winter, and never being
        the one that got away.

Skinbyrds

Tattooed by friends, the spittle of Hastings
in spring: my life, not much so far but a hard
look setting my face to read *working class pride.*
My hands stuffed in pockets or flicking some

endless cigarette. I'm with the other girls,
feathercut and sloping our spines against the brick,
all trucked up in heavy eyeliner and bright lips.
We're young enough to still be lovely things

no matter how hard the old siren screams
it's paddywagon song. So why are we standing
around, waiting for the boys to be interesting?
Look at them, shoving each other against cement

for fun and games, ladding down a back alley
wild as red fur, foxing about, hellbent
on a trick of the light and a five fingered discount.
And that one—scrap of silk in his pocket,

half rude boy, halfway handsome, all jumped up,
not trying too hard. He's going to come over now
and start blagging on about things we all know—
like coppers can't be trusted, and parents are a joke.

We know why we're here. We're waiting for our moment
to come, the chance to throw our arms
around the sun, the mace of our days,
and hunt down the good time that we're owed.

After Dark at the Tate Britain

Ghostly, *this Torso in Metal*:
cold dark matter explodes
inwards, a coterie
of dismembered carpentry,
post-tornado story of limbs.
Flashlight bobbing
about dark causeways,
sculpture after sculpture
navigated with echolocation.
The impressionists leave
none like this: Monet's
waterlilies dilute in the dark,
a beam across them yields
no depth. They live only
in bright rooms, light blue air.
Better to comb through
the many beards of Blake,
the brimstone a high contrast
sort of bleak. This is the hour
of traces, where your ear
picks up everything
your battery operated eye
does not: that banging
you hear has been interpreted
as a beating heart or a clock's
pendulum. If you knew
the way out you'd take it.

Performance Art

This isn't really me, you know. I'm not really
a waitress. I've come here to the Sunshine State,
rhizome on the American East, to give you
a performance. I'm here to set this diner ablaze
with my authentic citizenry, my cauterized ambitions.

See how well I bring eggs and bacon to a table
at which I do not really bring eggs and bacon.
If I mess up your coffee order, it's not really me
apologizing, or wiping down formica with a greying
rag. I'm an artist, the best you've ever seen,

and you don't even know it yet—the Banksy of waitressing,
of working class Floridian azure. See how well I play
the role of a young woman who gave up her aggrandized
dreams of fame, and I never even stepped
off a bus or did a screen test.

Soon they will come: the critics, the deciders, the darlings
of the New York art scene, and declare me the voice
of a new generation, that this is the only true art, how
the zephyr of the diner stage has atomized my performance
into a pure form, capable of being breathed in by anyone.

As I bring you a basket of fries, take note:
the art of this gesture is going to amaze.

The Woodsman

Exiled to the country, you fancied yourself
    a woodsman 'til your hands cracked and bled
  with the arc of the axe splitting logs
      by a sculpted woodpile.
The brick wall is yellow. It goes nowhere.
    And when you translate 'password'
  it means 'shame,' but every time you try
      again your hands stab at the landscape

and the trees shake with rain. Now you're untied,
    fetished to the edge of dis-ease
  and you write it down to pull out the humours.
      Throw open the door on the rinsed-out

concrete floors with thin carpets, the ants building
    elaborate castles within drywall.
  Look at the little fire in the woodstove: it means the deer
      circle the edges of your land,

which means they sense you have no gun.
    Please know that it wasn't always
  supposed to be fun—please know I
      know no better than this.

Letters from Georgia O'Keeffe

I.

I want to walk through my world here
with you. It is so clear, with an ages-old
feeling like the evening star, the many
lakes under the long hot sunset line.

It isn't just the place, but the life
that happens there—the Rio Grande,
the mountains, the pattern of rivers
like nothing else that ever grew.

The world all bright-cut like time
and history simplified and straightened.
I wonder what your days are like,
what we can spar about next.

I've been sleeping on the roof this week.
I like to see the sky when I wake and I like the air,
I like seeing all over my world with the rising sun.
I sometimes wish I'd never seen it, the pull is so strong.

II.

Your letter yesterday was tremendous—
I started to read it on the street, caught
my breath and stopped, put it back
in the envelope. That night I picked it up

and sat thinking. I've sat here a long time
—a dog barking, the night very still—
a train way off rumbling and humming.
It is cold and the crickets are singing.

When I think of you, I wish I could
put my hand on your shoulder
when you are alone. I'd like to give you
an airing in the country, blue sky

and water, clean flowers. Here
there is a whippoorwill and the air
is sweet with lilacs, the grass tall and soft,
it looks a bit deserted, but I like that.

Maybe that's why I want to touch
you so often—it's just another way of talking.
And I hate to be completely outdone
by a little thing like distance.

III.

There's one painting and flocks
of failures draped around me
in bunches. You see, I have frozen
in the mountains in the rain and hail,

cooked and burned my nose and arms
on the desert so that riding
through Kansas on the train
when everyone else is wilting

seems nothing at all for heat.
My nose has peeled and all my bones
are sore. I have felt like the lash
on a stinging whip, or a bridge

only wide enough for a single hip.
Sometimes it feels
like I'm working in the dark
but it's a work that must be done.

IV.

The flower is painted large to convey
my experience of the flower.
I have done nothing all summer
but wait to be myself again.

You must know that my coming out
to these toylike islands on the sea
is only an evasion. Flowers and birds,
all pretty things, light and lovely and nothing.

What is my experience of the flower
if not colour? No one makes any remarks
about your affairs, so I make none.
Anything I say is the same as if it wasn't said

at all—the words are just songs that a man
I have come to know is singing.
The feeling a person gives me
comes in colours and shapes—

I sat through dinner in a room without music
one night, thinking the center of you seems built
with your mind—clear, beautiful, relentless.
If I could go with my letter to you and the lake—

But this asks nothing of you.
You have other things to think of now.
What is my experience of a person
if it is not colour and shape.

V.

I sometimes wonder if I'm crazy to sit
down in a faraway country, but at least
it is quiet here. No radio, no newspaper.
I get vegetables and fruit from the ranch house

two miles away. I've only been to town
twice since I arrived, once to the morada,
a small long building on a hill well above
the town. Inside the walls a pale sweet pink

and an alter full of gory Christs and saints—
a startling figure in black with a bow
and arrow, 7 heavy crosses big enough
to crucify a man, a great iron chain, a wall

splattered with blood; the mixture of pain and love:
pain the implements of religion and love
in the care of the place. The mud and the cold
and rain and dust and wind drove me home

on Friday. I was too tired, too torn to threads
in town. The daylight is coming.
I am going up on the roof to watch it come.
We do such things here without being thought crazy.

A Classic Pack of Camel Cigarettes

Some days it feels like nothing
will ever change in this town,
other days it's a landscape
like the front of a classic pack
of camel cigarettes, exotic black
angles under a different sun.
We hunt for specifics, anything

overlooked in the ashed-out
twilight to claim our own:
bottle cap, earring, a piece
of blue glass worn opaque
by the beach, the novelty of egrets
mating in the green garden
your neighbour made after his wife

died in a five-car pileup.
Each spring as he turns the earth
he recalls the state trooper awkward
at his front door, describing
interstate constellations of car
parts scattered like satellites
that got lost on their way home.

The Legend of Zelda

*I wish I could write a beautiful book to break those
hearts that are soon to cease to exist: a book of faith
and small neat worlds and of people who live by the
philosophies of popular songs.*
—Zelda Fitzgerald

Is it so terrible that I want you to think my words
genius in their own gin-spilled right?
Oh, and a headband of feathers, rouge,
and six new dance steps to distract for the night.

I could write, if you gave me a triforce
smooth as zinc, and heartbreak
like we know best. I'll make up the lost letters,
let them link together in rings

of condensation where the glass still sweats.
Let's begin the rumour of a new affair
where an ocarina sings the song
your finger makes rimming the edge of a gimlet.

Maybe this time, we'll really be done with the party.
Then I could don a tiara of typewriter
keys and settle down to a desk
at the Skyloft hotel where I'll begin my high rule.

Sirens of the Deep Sea Mermaid Camp

The state bird of Florida is a northern mocking bird.

Above the water theatre, you'll practice dolphin
kicks and ballet, shimmying into a sequined
spandex tail and applique starfish bra.

[argon, neon, vapour. water without a treeline.]

Then submerged you'll be revealed in the belly
of a the glass sided pool, your hands full of serum,
turtles shunting faux pearls from the mermaids

before you, then a slow spin, your hair liquescent.

Your green tail flares under the lights
[with all the direction of milkweed seeds,
appearing everywhere and then lingering.]

You're tanked on the coolness of your own skin,
the way your hair expands and contracts
like a myth around you, the silver fish flashing

like cutlery at this banquet of artificial coral,

imported sand [your hands—hummingbirds
darting over the water,
suddenly capable of producing ultraviolet light.]

Soon the prop anchor rises and falls

as you become a tattoo, the totem at a bow
of a ship crossing oceans in search of spices,
or deep green plastic necessary

to become the you you paid $400 dollars to be.

The Barbers of Rotterdam

"this isn't just a job, it's a lifestyle-
we dress like barbers, we live like barbers."
        —Coos, Schorem Barbers Documentary

A good haircut is the art of negative space,
an ear exposed as a diamond. To live
like a barber is to love the trimmed hair
that falls from your sleeves like cinnamon
into coffee, salt onto steak. Even
the clientele are happy to have a few
of their own trimmings floating in beer,
the Pinaud-Clumbman aftershave infused
like gin. As far as scumbags go,
these illustrated men are quite grand—
the kind that make a good living pomadeing
moustaches, drawing new portraits
with straight razors, muttering incantations
for manliness into the sound system.

Sainthood

Backlit into sainthood, wine glasses
make out in the cabinet.

We have loved in their expanse,
lakeside and skyscraper.

Once I found a photograph in your desk
of a woman who looked like me—

her dress glowed in the camera's
flash, the champagne flute aloft

in the foreground, imperfect smile
caught mid-laugh. Who was she?

Her pale hands became violin bows
that strummed my nervous system.

When I went back to look again,
she was gone. As though she got up

out of the drawer and walked away.
As though your desk

were a hotel room where she lived
briefly, never to return again.

Wishing is Easier than Being

I dreamt of a stadium lit up
with pyrotechnics,
flashing beams of cobalt
over ecstatic faces
before waking to your voice
saying I should really do
something with my day.

Clouds of oleander crowd
the front door—leaving
is to risk the bees that rule them.
Wishing is easier than being,
travelling without the drudgery
of travel. Imagining stories
without having to live them.

I can waste a swimming pool
of days doing nothing,
never once booking a flight.
Why should I? Sleep brings
me to the ankles of the Pyrenees,
their rivers of melted snow
and wild herbs, patiently waiting

for miracles I can almost touch.

Dorothy and the First Tornado

The sky is greening, foaming
like the top of a bubbling pot.
And look, see how the clouds

climb down to dance with us?
How the animals rush up to meet
them, and conduct the thrashing sounds?

The clouds want to circle
on their own, thick rounds
across the fields, growing near.

Shingles, rakes, shovels through
the air—so many things
learning to fly, or could they do

this all along? Come down
from the sky, you silly cows.
Come back to the barn, blown open.

II. LADY CRAWFORD

Lady Crawford

Sputnik chandeliers, beige walls for days:
there's a hotel in your head, halls paced
like the fractured asterisk of the union
jack. In luxurious countries we are fenced
in with wainscoting and a lineage of earls
stretching back to the thirteen hundreds,
all the Lady Crawfords before me. Our
peerage tweed a rugged veil between each,
lined up not always for slaughter, but some
to rule our little fifedoms with aplomb.
Here in my castle, a condo on the west side,
give me a lake ready to envelop anyone
who dares enter. Give me the brainy
scattershot conversation of your friends
best-impressing their latest acquisitions,
their new sure things, while I practice humility.
Who am I to interfere? There is no reprieve.
Hail to the Lindsay plaid, Clan Crawford,
Hail to Lady after Lady of the luckless empire.

Have Fun Storming the Castle

The house knows it needs a moat, but there's none to be found.
The boxwood shrubs decorate when they need to protect.
The front door is glossy but repels nothing but rain.
The local hockey team patrols an indoor ice rink, dreams of winning.

The others, they have dreams of better lives that don't exist.
Their lives are the better ones, where they can yearn and reach.
Things don't give us anything but order, a single use tool.
The single use tools all need a place, lest they overrun us with their thingness

The right kitchen tile will bring you inner peace.
The new quest for meaning yielded moisture-wicking technology.
The secular world is falling short, lacks the shine we know and love.
The stoicism of our worldview is no match for the enthusiasm for change.

The ones without: they hear birdsong of lit-up things, and come for you.
They march on your home and terrify the boxwoods, rend the glossy door.
The violence will be unfair, but measured—they need it.
Flowers ripped to pieces and the smash of glass singing.

Bloodshed is variable, depending on how prepared you are.
The limits of things will be expanded, dispersed like atoms.
The disbursement will leave your family cowering in a safe room.
The enthusiasm will save some lives, but not yours.

The Sermon from the Lexus

This traffic, in which we're all corralled, is exhausting.
Pulsing turning signal, save me from the hoi polloi,
here and on my way back home. Let the people
have pulp novels and McDonald's, mass market
everything. Give me this day my GPS coordinates,
e-cigarettes, takeout meals and internet porn;
and deliver me from myself, as we deliver others
with compliments and coffee. I'll forgive myself
the dalliance, the harsh bite at my daughter
with arguments against bedtimes, as all the magazines
say I should—after all, I'm only one woman.
Lead me not into the idea that I could do better,
for truly I can not. For mine is the kingdom of yoga's
mountain pose, retinol creams that keep me
looking ten years younger, the crossfit and detox
salads that keep me trim, forever and ever. Amen.

On Origins

You weren't born into nobility.

One-room basement apartment,
single mother, public schools
and spaghetti dinners.

Dresses hand-sewn at a time
when store-
bought was in fashion.

Years before your plainness
gave way to fine
bones, learned artistry.

You went on to live many places

each a rope you wove yourself.
It was decades before
you came to learn your fingerprint

is your address,
that property value is inversely
proportional to how real home feels.

Lord Crawford

You believe in single malt
sweetening the worst of it.

You love the smoothness
of the lacquered wood,

the smell of my perfume
(linden and laurel)

as though I were a patch
of grass and flowers

in which to bury your hands,
the zippered length

of my back. Because I am
a thing, am I not?

A terrarium, a ring, a gold
coin. And you, can you

see your own thing-ness—
buttoned down shirt,

haircut, a driverless car
sonic down the highway?

Sometimes when we kiss
the highway shifts

its lanes so we can make
our exit, a near miss

that leaves hands pressed
to the wheel's center,

trumpets sounding all around us.

Money Dogs

Dream you have swallowed
the stark art of each ordinal,
and strolled mercenary

around the market floor,
your name an oracle
for denominators while black

phones purr in digital tones.
How does it feel?
Like champagne sabred

into a fount of achievement,
foaming carbon centrifuging
a flute? Like bedding men

stripped of fine suits, each ego
nested in the company
shredder's daily offerings?

Like five seconds of breath
and then it's on to the next
to amortise, leverage, and sketch

out a carnival of spending
in margins that will turn us all
into merchandise, pink

shrimp on crushed white ice?
Our sombre cartel eyeing
numbers, like mongrels
who have done without for days.

Lineage: Hugh and Margaret Crawford (1195-1265)

This is what I know: The Chief of Clan Crawford was like every other father. Ambition bred not in the bone but in the fervent dinner conversations with his wife, suggesting that things would be better if the Norse would bugger off already. He baited and led them until October, when the fall shores gave way to storms and their ships were no match for the rough seas of Scotland. To the confused Norsemen dying on the shore, arrows were a kind of weather.

The Uncrawfording

Any coupling is a taunt,
a bitten thumb searching
for someone to insult.

By what measures
did my husband's
sisters consider their vows?

Were they as simple
and impulsive
as mine? I gambled.

Took a boy of good breeding
and bet his stock
would rise, his very company

like a place I went to work.
Marriage is always
an investment, a bond bought

lock-and-barrel;
but if they could shed
their Crawford crests

let me tell you something
I've never told
anyone—his name fits me

like a wedding dress.

At the Investment Firm Christmas Party

It is good to have money, finally. I've claimed Warren Buffett
as my patron saint, and if someone has to have more,
then why not me? I'm happy to raise my sidecar
and slide good fortune's hand into mine, praise
the deciding stars, who saw this coming with a youth misspent.

There are others like me—entered the stock market, married well,
interrogated their investments to the point of cruelty, flourished
like bonsais. Others claim to be too artistic for success
but hold firm to dream of fame that will one day dismount
off the mangy back of verse, and welcome them.

Having money, like anything else, is a malleable art.
Not that struggling sort of game, where we're all trying
to write like the men we imagine, and the men we imagine
are vaulted further into a canon of idealism
like the hairless pubis of Botticelli's Venus and Michelangelo's

fresh-from-the-pool discreet penis. But there are casualties:
I will miss crossing lawns, carrying a case of beer to a party,
I will miss gambling when buying a sweater that cost
more than thirty dollars. Now my living string of numbers
grows fat and fatter still, like pandas at the zoo with nothing

to do but eat and sleep out of boredom. My nightmare:
the plush account turns its numeric eye on me
and throws stock symbols back like a curtain as if to say,
oh I'm sorry, this never really belonged to you. I'm just the married guy
flirting with you by the buffet, I'm going home with somebody else.

On Origins II

My absent father was an Elvis-

loving mechanic, broken
down car collector,
cheap beer connoisseur.

Every single idea
he had was the next big thing
that never came.

Each schoolyard friend

was smarter and prettier than me,
understood the social
aquarium in which we swam

like a second skin.
I dreamt of recording
generic pop songs,

tapping at a small plastic
keyboard on cloud mapped
days I never understood.

Lineage: Ron and Mary Crawford

This is what I know: He tried before the war, but she wouldn't have him. He went away to finishing school, which war could sometimes be. She learned to sew and how to best butcher a hen. He was a gunner in a ball turret, and shot down anything that wasn't a bird. She knit socks for the front, rationed sugar, wanted adventures of her own. She slept in a bed with a floral quilt. War was a plague, contagious and airborne. Forests bore witness, girls went to work and with the men mostly gone, she finally felt free. He learned how to get a haircut that suited him. When he returned in his uniform and sharp grey overcoat, smelling of Mennen cologne, they courted with the clear-eyed romance of survivors. When they married, he wore his RAF uniform and she carried a book of prayers. They completed crossword puzzles, he learned architecture and went to work for a firm. She kept the home, the way women were supposed to. Her legs started to falter. He became an expert at toast and tea. They made a garden, English bonsai, gravel paths. They both had curly hair. They had two children, and clung to each other like damp cotton.

Happy Families

We sit in the dining room
and watch the rain come,

its grey good looks
whipping the bushes.

How the green deepens
the moment you lower

your newspaper to Sunday's
roast, or small sandwiches

taken for tea. Himalayan
pink salt, Tuscan olives,

a fridge full of precious
jam jars. You've another

hour before a conference
call with the New York

office, the space between
now and then

a rose of discontent, blooming.

Cottage Still Life, with Barbecue

I am full of hope, and gin.
The afternoon's only redeeming
qualities are that the drinks
keep coming, and the men went off
to bore each other with their
small accomplishments.

                                   I am full of hope,
                                   and did I mention the gin,
                                   I'm filled to the bloody brim

with the smothering comfort
of a cottage as rustic as a five star resort,
flowers that bloom on command
in their jaunty pots that coordinate
with the patio furniture.

I want to want.
And I want for not.   Except-

                                   Are the steaks done yet?

The boat-borrowing neighbours
insist we turn on the TV
for updates on the middle east—
news cameras poke at the delicate corpse
of a woman surrounded by shining gore
seeping into a white bedsheet.

Someone always says, *turn that off, I'm trying to enjoy myself.*

The trying is what gets me.
It's like, the discomfort.

Can't we talk about something else?

Of course.

But let's face it—no one wants to say
aloud how the rockets eviscerating
some other country fills you with relief
because you're glad it isn't your children's
limbs scattered like bread we toss to birds.
Where does the news anchor linger—
Syria, Nigeria, the Gaza strip?

Who's ready for another drink?

It's so far away, you say,
and here in the lake-lit calm
three martinis in, men
clustered around the barbecue poking
at steaks with long metal tongs,
you are at peace.

III. FIGHT OR FLIGHT

Fight or Flight

In some countries, a daughter
is fear made flesh.

Once there was movie about college girls
clad in bikinis and pink ski
masks, clutching berettas
in Florida's manic orange juice sun.
Soon, all the men are dead
and the girls, sexual as overkill,
drive off in a Lamborghini.

Not unlike the onna-bugeisha—
Samurai women wielding a naginata,
defending their homes and children
and honour from marauders
while their husbands were away at war.

Young girls taught
the loft of a sword so long
it pulled horsemen from the air
and thrashed them to roses.

Cassadaga Spiritualist Camp

Herons and egrets are signs,
vultures too. Nothing to bestow
upon you but lucky nickels
and a sense of déjà vu.

How is it that every visitor
who finds their long lost ghost
begins to manifest
in the blue orchards

of readers, palms and cards?
The heat makes you dizzy,
or is that the rush of your past
running up to meet you?

The locket your grandmother hid.
Your father's childhood scar.
A woman in a fingertip illusion veil.
The intake of breath.

Tapestry: Minerva in Battle

Mind-hatched, fully
formed as a wish—
I'm dateless and I
don't care. The owls
are what I love,
their aviary
of feathers and snow
and wood chips.

In the morning
when they're sleeping,
it's toast at the table
and the sullen day
of work ahead of me—
battlefields
worn down to velvet
under regular handling.

I'll put the coffee on
and get to work—
I coined the phrase
don't quit your day job
so I don't. I work until
the weaving that depicts
the owls' victory
is nearly a prayer.

Happy Birthday

This is a happy birthday.

You can tell by the fringed tinsel garland, beloved by used car lots
that had their heyday in the Eighties.

You can step into a happy birthday by selecting a location
and telling friends and family to show up.

All happy birthdays are alike—
The clink of glasses, the laughter boiling to a shriek.

But unhappy birthdays are different.

Too much drink, too few friends,
family scattered so time differences render their messages obsolete.

The one person you most want to hear say *Happy Birthday*
never calls or shows up.

The cards are full of fart jokes.
No one knows your favourite kind of cake.

And where are the candles, shining their short lived radiance
on your awkward face?

Is that what the year gets you, every time?

The Flu

Your follicles sing their torment
as though pain were the woman
you loved most dropping
her robe to the floor in a pool
of glass. Running without
moving, surging along
with the disorder that lays you
down in your bed and says: *rest.*
You'll know when I'm done with you.

Horses for Courses

When you say 'it's gonna happen now'
Well, when exactly do you mean?
See I've already waited too long
And all my hope is gone.
                    —The Smiths, "How Soon is Now?"

I've seen you threadbare, my back-pocket
has-been. Here in the pub when we could have stayed
locked in my flat; counterspied, stupefied.
The afternoon both contracting and opening.
Once, I found your underwear on the floor,
breathed it in and thought it delicious. Go
ahead, tell everyone we know that we
won't advertise our indifference, that a pairing
like this is as sure as horses for courses,
and *when you say 'it's gonna happen now'*

I'll have arguments against sense,
against the days where I'm sure of what
I want. It's only when you're not around
I see the rock you chained yourself to,
the bird that pecks your liver. I want you
when you're at your most extreme,
a ranting demi-god amoung empty pints.
Pubs a thousand years in the same place
tell us we can get used to anything.
Well, when exactly do you mean?

I'm drunk, dressed in white fox fur
and dying to hold your hand. I'm judging
everyone here: men too cavalier,
and women trying not to care. Ask them
why it matters, and they'll dissolve
into snakes before you. Lapse of shirt, lapse
of lyrics. I'll quote off-the-cuff fragments,
bridge your unravelling reasons
until you're drunk too and covered
in ellipses. *See I've already waited too long,*

so tell me again why we're here
when we could be at your flat, untethered,
lawless. Not bucked by hindsight's long
strides, but rinsed with cigarettes
and every reason to be alone.
You bend your voice over my shoulders
until the fields bleed green and I'm laying down
in slick barracks, hill-backed and dripping
with sorrys. You say nothing, walk out
smoking, *and all my hope is gone.*

Every Book is a Self Help Book

The books are a stopgap,
a time delay mechanism
filled with affirmations
for charting your own way
through the desert of happiness,
to scale the face of god.

Some borrow the glow
of Rumi, quotes tarted up
in handwritten fonts,
digitally added watercolours.
Stop striving. Plug into the universe.
It's a new New Age.

*

Another day sped by lakes
before being tossed off
a ponderosa motorcycle,

another night drinking
the wine of strangers
and bedding down
their own sour breath.

Big Che and Little Che,
each loved a girl back home,
but distance dilutes beauty,
dilutes the come-back call.

*

Surely there are still
leper colonies somewhere.
I could go, ride a motorcycle
over minor roads,

chant mantras
for good vibrations.
I would pour my light
into the empty cups

of lepers, and be whole.

*

Or I could live with a muster
of peacocks strutting
their flower-eating style
through the sun's audience.

The universe in bird form,
tails mapping galaxies,
colours the base
element of pigment.

*

Is it possible to love another
if you have stared into the blue neck
of a peacock for more than an hour?
Sometimes their eyes,
both real and feathered,
stalk my thoughts, their chicken feet
scratching at the sheets.

*

Big Che and Little Che fill their pockets
with dirt, the idea they
will change the Americas.

Where to find their names,
their speciality, other than
penning the hitchhiker's

guide to mooching
on a drifting, bee-staggered
route to the colonies?

It's only romantic if you
revolt in a lush green
country that charms the mind.

*

Another hour. Then another.
The day eaten like a flower

faster than you can
get your thoughts down.

The day stalking off
in the mouths of birds.

*

I once loved a bracelet
so much it ceased to exist.
Like how when you stare
at a particular star, it diminishes.

*

We plan poorly then declare
ourselves 'spontaneous', which
feels like a German word for
"I want to live my life without
deciding what I actually want".
Could I still tumble through
South America on a motorbike
held together with wire
and good intentions, stealing
onto boats that might be heading
to some newly discovered island?

*

Above the hen house, a peacock
rests in a pulpit of branches.
Sometimes its squawk in the night
is pure siren, emergency in progress.

Sometimes it is the sound
of a dream being cleaved.
But if this dream is gone,
will another come to take its place?

The peacock judged it faulty,
sings by snapping sticks into threes.

*

What am I to strive for now?
A lost bracelet, an adventure
to pen a bestseller?

Like a motorbike kicking
up rough gravel
on the back road route,

I'm just sound calling out
the universe, begging it
to do what it wants.

Minerva Leaves the Temple

When the drunks toddle off
to their taxis and stagger
onto the side walk, I make my way
back to the forest, sober as a bell.
Now that the sky is a cool
dark hand on my forehead,
I can shake the glitter
from my hair. There are battles

and tapestries to plan out
tomorrow. I park my car
at the edge of the woods
and leave the windows rolled
down. May the sword strike
the shield and the earth,
but never bone.
May the battle be precise

as the prayers of owls.
Who owns who?
Who believes in the old gods?
Let's be glamourous,
sinews shining with sweat,
shrews baiting across a field.
Under, and then further under
the moon's white tablecloth eye.

Letter from Egon Schiele

The city is black, everything
done by recipe.
Let them regard me
with dissembling eyes.

I want to visit the forest,
taste dark waters, the crash
of trees and untamed air
and cellar-scented earth.

I want to hear the evening's
cool breathing,
and the gnats singing
like wires in the wind.

I traversed the wet roads,
I went through until March.
Today I believe I am someone
completely different.

Groupies

Most won't understand and it's hard
to explain, but attention seeking is the new kind
of proxied fame—costumed in vintage
before vintage was cool, the margin
where legions are eyelinered
into cartoons—the notorious spectacle
that cuts our senses to confetti
and our impossible selves carry on stage
until the music stops and we stand
undancing, pinned into place by the truth
that our lives might not actually matter,
then throw our hands up in the air,
gut the horizon with our red nails
and let fruit punch light bleed the night out.

Bess Houdini

1.

The ring on my hand is a sparkler alright,
a rich old lady ring I'll grow
into as the years swell and I harden,
carbonized into a jewel of a wife.
It's a magician's trick: put a girl
in a box, abracadabra her into marriage.

It is better before beginning, better
than the warbled little muster we pass
off as art. Is there anything worse
than what if? An illusion falling flat?
The simplest gestures are serrated
with other thoughts, photographs.

It's the posterity that scares us.
We might become adventurers,
more interesting and better looking;
we might lose everything.
A love story gone on too long
and devoid of tragedy
has the crowd in yawns.

2.

I don't know if it's going as well
as I thought, I don't know
how it's supposed to go.

You're shirtless at the ironing
board, pressing the collar
of your button up down.

I'm standing at the door,
looking at you like I've never
seen you before:

husband of many years,
partner in, enemy against,
happiness.

3.

You look up and see your wife,
the person disguised as me:

tall as west coast foxglove,
loved like a cult classic film.

On a good day, this is enough.

Sunrise with Sea Monsters

Tourists, the seashore is nothing
more than a dirty mile
of horizon and the smell of fish
tacos clinging to our clothes.

Who will be the last alive
to share this view?
The ten carat gold sky,
its mustard gas dream.

Let's find a handsome cab
and tell the driver to drive
around until the meter
hits sixty and the horses tire,

the sun forever rising
on the British empire,
dragging its gamey leg
around town.

Minerva Among the Owls

It isn't their eyes, but the way they turn them on
at night. The beautiful one is Alabaster.
The one with the hard luck
is my favourite, the way he flies.
That one with the chipped beak, Parthenon.
Afterfeathered, full of hark-ness.

Unspooled ribbons, nightclub light. Arms out and up
in this dark box beating the head of everyone
with the pulse in my wrists. I could do this all night, unlearn
the day, my name nothing more than a tourist fountain.
It's a dance club remix, all reverb and sedation.

When Hard Luck died,
I was dancing in a strobe light as I held
a skipping rope and lassoed whorls in the air.
I arrived in a taxi, took him into my stark arms.
The others came to gather, fold his talons closed
and fill his beak with sequins.

They are and are not what they seem:
heads like a bowlful of flour,
faces like car alarms, harbingers, bright moths.
Here in the shadow of a mirrorball,
their eyes punch holes straight through you.

Moon over cypress trees, cedarleaf.

Notes

"Letters from Georgia O'Keeffe" is based on found fragments in the letters of Georgia O'Keeffe.

"After Dark at The Tate Britain" refers to an art competition where the winning design was a robot that could be remote controlled via the Internet, and would roam the gallery at night, shining a flashlight on various works of art.

The "Lady Crawford" suite is a fictionalized reimagining of several members of my husband's family lineage, including myself. Fun fact: the Crawford lineage includes Mary Crawford, the mother of Scottish hero William Wallace.

"Self Help" was inspired by an eclectic reading of *The Motorcycle Diaries* by Ernesto Guevara, Flannery O'Connor's Essay "The King of Birds", and *Light is the New Black* by Rebecca Campbell.

"Letter from Egon Schiele" contains found fragments from Mr. Schiele's poems and letters.

"Sunrise with Sea Monsters" is inspired by the painting of the same name by J.W.M. Turner.

Acknowledgements

My thanks to the editors of the following publications where poems in *Lady Crawford* previously appeared: *Contemporary Verse 2, Grain, The Fiddlehead,* and *Taddle Creek.*

"Sunrise with Sea Monsters" was published on sunrisewithseamonsters. blogspot.com, an exphrastic poetry blog created and curated by Paul Vermeersch.

"Skynbirds" received an honourable mention in *The Fiddlehead*'s 2014 Ralph Gustafson Poetry Competition.

My gratitude to the excellent team at Palimpsest Press, particularly Aimee Parent Dunn, Dawn Kresan, and to my editor and friend, Jim Johnstone. Many thanks to my husband, Guy Crawford, for his unwavering support of this book—both the concept and the time needed to write it.

The Ontario Arts Council provided funding for this project through the Writer's Reserve Program.

About the Author

Julie Cameron Gray is originally from Sudbury, Ontario. She is the author of *Tangle* (Tightrope Books, 2013), and two chapbooks: *The Distance Between Two Bodies* (Cactus Press, 2006) and *Coordinating Geometry* (Emergency Response Unit, 2010). Her work has been previously published in *Carousel, Event, The Fiddlehead, Prairie Fire, PRISM International,* and *The Best Canadian Poetry in English.* She currently lives in Toronto.